TAKING BACK MY YESTERDAYS

TAKING BACK MY YESTERDAYS

Linda H. Hollies

The Pilgrim Press
Cleveland, Ohio

lessons in forgiving and moving forward with your life

The Pilgrim Press, Cleveland, Ohio 44115
© 1997 by Linda H. Hollies

Art on pages ii and xxx by Sheila Williams; used by permission
of the artist. Text by Jacqueline Ford and Deborah Tinsley
Taylor used by permission of the authors. "Taking Back My
Yesterdays" used by permission of Valerie J. Bridgeman Davis.
From *Psalms Anew: In Inclusive Language,* compiled by Nancy
Schreck and Maureen Leach, © 1986 by Saint Mary's Press.
Used by permission of the Saint Mary's Press, Winona,
Minnesota. All rights reserved. From *Julian of Norwich: Showings*
by Edmund Colledge, O.S.A., and James Walsh, S.J.,
© 1978 by the Missionary Society of St. Paul the Apostle in the
State of New York. Used by permission of Paulist Press,
Mahwah, New Jersey.

02 01 00 99 98 97   5 4 3 2 1

Library of Congress Cataloging-in-Publication Data

Hollies, Linda H.
    Taking back my yesterdays : lessons in forgiving and moving
forward with your life / Linda H. Hollies.
        p.   cm.
    Includes bibliographical references.
    ISBN 0-8298-1208-3 (pbk. : alk. paper)
    1. Forgiveness—Religious aspects—Christianity. I. Title.
BV4647.F55H65 1997
234′.5—dc21   97-25343
                                                        CIP

This book is dedicated to the sisters of Woman to Woman Ministries. These are a group of God-sent sisters who have loved me through periods of time when I needed to frequently engage these principles of forgiveness!

May God forever bless and keep my daughters in ministry, Jacqui Ford, Darlene Webster, Sandi Adams Cheryl Williams, Belyinda Johnson, and Tracy Flagg; my big sisters at Southlawn Community UMC in Chicago, Patricia Wilson, Lonnie Simmons, Carrie Holt, Lucille Jones, Jeannie Wilder, and Gwen Peters; my prayer-warrior, encourager sisters, Rev. Daisybelle Thomas-Quinney, Dr. Janet Hopkins, Dr. Linda Boston, Rev. Lillian Gibbs, Rev. Harlene Harden, Rev. Michelle Cobb, Rev. Beverly Garvin, Dr. Valerie Bridgeman Davis, Rev. Genevieve Brown; my sister pastor Rev. Eleanor Miller, my mother-sister Lucille Brown, and my butterfly sister-friends Vera Jo Edington and Rev. Joyce Wallace. Without them my journey could have been stuck in yesterday!

I am blessed with sister poets in my life. They gift me with words of inspiration, prose, and truth. I give God thanks for bringing both Valerie Bridgeman Davis and Deborah Tinsley Taylor into my life. It is a privilege to share some brief excerpts of their poetry with you. They write from their soulful experiences and push us into better tomorrows. Thanks Deb! Thanks Val!

CONTENTS

PREFACE

The idea of writing a book on forgiveness did not simply come to me! It arrived via my telephone. Author Iyanla Vanzant and I had shared several telephone calls where we talked about the journey to wholeness. Both of us had real live stories to detail our war wounds along the way. I had just recently put my story on paper for all the world to see with the release of *Inner Healing for Broken Vessels*.

Six years later, Iyanla Vanzant agent Denise Stinson approached her about writing a book on the need for forgiveness. Ilyana referred her to me! On that December afternoon as Denise and I shared conversation, I knew that this was God's way of speaking to my heart:

Linda, as you journey to inner healing
and wholeness, it's essential that you
release unto me those who have hurt
you. As you teach others about taking
steps which will free them from old,
painful garbage, it's fundamental that
you include the keys to forgiveness. For
without forgiveness, the "old stuff"
keeps its tentacles wrapped around your
heart! Without forgiveness, inner healing can never be complete.

Questions were raised in my own mind
about my process to forgiving and releasing.
Old issues emerged as I entered into my own
personal prayer closet. I had to engage the little
girl within me and check out how she felt
about forgiving and moving ahead with life.
Memory played out her role as I relived some
scenes from my past.

The old clips from yesterday rolled by and I saw how I used to be. Swiftly I watched the video of my life. I saw pain. I relived hurt. I felt anger. I shed more tears. And I experienced grace. I discovered that I was not held captive by what had happened yesterday. There was today, and there was tomorrow.

On the very day that Denise called me, the title of this book was birthed as I sat in prayer. *Taking Back My Yesterdays!* For it's something I must will to do. The enemy of our soul will not give back our yesterdays without a struggle. But Scripture has already declared, "The Realm of God has been advancing forcefully and the righteous *take it by force*" (Matthew 11:12, emphasis added).

There are keys to unlocking your heart to forgiveness. There are scriptural principles which must be acknowledged, learned, and applied if you intend to move from yesterday.

There are some lessons God would have us learn and share as we move ahead into the promise of tomorrow.

I pray you take back your yesterdays! My Baptist brother Rev. Donald Sharp's church, Faith Tabernacle in Chicago, taught me a song of victory for those who are determined to engage yesterday and snatch it back.

> I went into the enemy's camp
> and I took back what was stole from me!
> I took back what was stole from me!
> I took back what was stole from me!
> I went into the enemy's camp
> and I took back what was stole from me!
> Now the enemy's under my feet,
> under my feet, under my feet, under my
>   feet,
> for ain't no devil in hell going to walk on
>   me!

The key biblical principle for me is taken from Proverbs 6:31: whatever the enemy stole from you must be repaid seven times over! You get ready to multiply your joy, your delight, your peace, your satisfaction, your progress, your healing, and your wholeness as you and God reclaim all of your stolen yesterdays!

SHALOM, MY FRIENDS,
SISTER LINDA

ACKNOWLEDGMENTS

A book is never written in isolation. All the persons who touch, influence, inspire, and even hinder your life help you in the writing process. The lessons you have learned and the individuals who taught you hover over your shoulders, waiting to see if you have mastered the materials. In the same way that "it takes a village to raise a child," it takes your entire life community to write a book.

I'm thankful to my life community for my personal experiences and awareness of the journey of forgiveness. Many are the charitable and gracious souls who have forgiven me when I have stumbled, blundered, and just plain messed up! I have been picked up, lifted up, forgiven, and blessed to grow and to become by my life community.

My family of origin heads the list of folks who helped to write this book. My grandmothers—Lucinda Weston, Eunice Wade, Ethel Kellom, and Lessie Bell King—live in me, speak to me, and continue to admonish and cheer me as they watch from the realms of glory. My Big Daddy, Dock Wade, is with them and I appreciate the loving role model he provided. My parents, James and Doretha Adams, gave me life and granted me the necessary lessons that have taught me to hold on to God's unchanging hand! My aunt, Barbara Weston, taught me, by example, the art of meditation, relaxing, releasing, and letting go of yesterday's pain. All of these dear people now await me on the other side. I simply pray that I teach their lessons well.

My siblings and extended family are the rich soil that has nurtured my soul. For Jacquie,

Bob, and Troy; Riene, Tony, Lynne, Michael, and Missy; Regina, Arthur, Raymond, Ibn, and Millicient; James Jr., Jeanette, Noah, and Mohanna; Eddie, Onnette, Eddie Jr., and Candace; David, Kim, Dave Jr., and Ean; and Robert Tyrone, I give God thanks and praise.

Finally, my husband Chuck, my daughter Grian, her sons Giraurd and Gamel, my sons Greg and Grelon have each taught me lessons and learned because of me how to love and to forgive. My family is another name for love!

INTRODUCTION

This story starts like most of our stories begin, with a group of women. We gathered the first Saturday of the month for two hours to talk about our lives as women. We had a topic to focus us. But, as conversations have a life of their own, our sharing took us in many directions.

We had an issue before us, for it was December, and the holidays were fast approaching. How could we beat the holiday blues? What could we intentionally do, or not do, to avoid the depression, anger, resentment, and pain which holidays can bring?

A group of women, varied in age, marital status, career paths, and economic range, came to share. From different parts of the city, from various denominations, and from a wide range of theological positions, we met to support each other. We simply talked woman to woman.

We brought in an "expert" to do a presentation and facilitate our discussion. And we recognized that she was simply another sister with additional information. For she's been in our shoes and is continuing the search for herself. So we fed each other and feasted from the diversity of our lives.

"What's your memory of your favorite Christmas?" Answers poured forth.

"My brother came home and I gave him a scarf I had made. He was so pleased."

"I was sixteen and working for the first time. I had money to buy small tokens for each one of my eleven siblings. They were overjoyed. I experienced the pleasure of giving."

"My mom had been away for a long time. She came home for Christmas."

"I finally had a child. I bought Pumpkin everything! My joy came from watching him open his gifts."

"I was sixteen and got a bad mouton fur!"

We all laughed. We all rejoiced. We all listened.

"What's the memory of your most awful Christmas?" There was silence. Hands reached into purses for tissues. Eyes closed. Heads began to nod. Hands reached out to one another for support as memories grabbed us and emotions carried us back to that pain, that place, that horror, and that fear.

"There was no man, no job, and no money. I had two sons. I had them cut out pictures of what they wanted and I gave them IOUs."

"I had decided no more of the physical abuse. He was gone. But as I walked down the aisle of a department store, I was overwhelmed with this sudden sadness. I had no man to buy a gift for."

"There had been this huge family fight. No one wanted to talk. There was no family gathering that year."

"It was the month before Christmas. He flunked the drug test and lost his job. I had to face the fact that he was an addict. I was pregnant with our second child."

We all experienced the memories. We all shared the hurt. We all listened. We all heard. And we all cried.

Here is where the story takes on new life. This is where our journey took another twist. For instead of simply wallowing in those painful memories, we decided to look at them, return to the pain, forgive the past, and *take back our yesterdays!*

Taking back a yesterday involves the willing decision to return to the place of pain. It means that you will confront the people involved in the painful situation, whether alive or dead. It

means that you allow the healing power of forgiveness to enfold you and the memory. And it
means that you will look at the other side of the
story through the compassionate Heart of Love.

Letting go of yesterday's pain takes the
power and the energy you have expended on
hating and hurting and puts it to work for you
on the journey toward healing and wholeness.
Forgiveness is an essential and primary building
block for all of us who want to live fruitful,
effective, and productive lives. Forgiveness is
always required for a life to move forward.
Forgiveness is the fundamental characteristic of
the universe. Without forgiveness, we have no
bridge to lead us to health and wholeness.

The writings of 1 John 1:8–9 remind us of
our need to take time and work on this issue of
forgiveness by declaring: "If we say, 'We are free
of the guilt of sin,' we deceive ourselves; the
truth is not to be found in us. But if we

acknowledge our sins, the one who is just can be trusted to forgive our sins and cleanse us from every wrong." As difficult as you will discover the journey to forgiveness to be, always remember the Love that forgives you, over and over again.

The key reason you will work on forgiveness is not for the individual who wronged you. The primary purpose of working on forgiveness is to release yourself from the grips of old hurting and haunting "stuff" that is blocking the good of the universe from coming your way. Unforgiveness hinders your blessings. Holding onto resentments and grudges causes the pathway to your fulfillment to be obstructed. When you can let go of the old pain in yesterday, you will be able to grasp all that the Divine has in store for you today!

This book is not intended to be read straight through quickly. For maximum benefit, each chapter needs to be read for at least seven days. However, I know that this is asking a lot from folks who have grown accustomed to the culture of "This instant, right now!" Therefore, my suggestion is that you begin each morning for a week by reading the prayer, psalm, and principle beginning your current chapter and pondering its meaning for your life. This will not be a quick trip. As deep as our pain and anger at old wounds has grown within us is how long it will take to unravel those tentacles, work through the mess, and prepare our hearts for the seed of forgiveness to be planted. Forgiveness is not an issue which you can rush in order to say, "Been there! Done that! Got the T-shirt!" You can get ready for an extended journey through a quiet storm which will change your life for the better.

Let a chapter with its prayer, psalm, and principle begin your day. Let them sink into

your spirit and work in your unconscious.
Chew on the principles. Digest them. Wrestle
with them. Struggle with them. Grapple with
what you will, won't, can't, and can do with the
process of forgiving. Pray the prayers if you can.
Add your own prayers. Meditate on the psalms
which have brought peace to the people of God
over the years. You may want to keep a journal
of your reflections, questions, and contempla-
tions as you read this book. Chronicle your
movement and growth, both for the days ahead
and for sharing with others when you are able.

One of the ways that the enemy of our
souls keeps us bound and chained in yesterday
is by causing us to forget the growth and the
movement we have already made in life. We
continue to take two steps forward and then
five steps back because the "good word" has
been snatched from our memory. So we write
it down in order to make the vision of who we

can become a plain reality in our subconscious mind. We write it down so that we can chart the movement, celebrate the growth, and "see" ourselves into a new and brighter tomorrow.

The prayers and psalms are only thought-joggers and affirmations to help "plant" the principle within your spirit. In your journal you may want to write letters to yourself and to the person you need to forgive. In this way you allow the "garbage" to get outside of you! For as you begin to empty out, the Holy Spirit can begin to fill you up again! Write a dialogue with God. This is how David wrote his Psalms. Now you can write yours. Perhaps you need to doodle. The work of our subconscious memory can allow a doodle to take on a life of its own and render many clarifying insights. So, wherever you might be, in a quiet space, on the bus, at your desk, stuck in traffic, or sitting on the "throne," remember that there is no spot where

God is not! And wherever God is there is the possibility for another new beginning

AUTHOR'S NOTE ABOUT SCRIPTURES

I take great personal liberty with Scripture! I believe it was written for me. And I know it needs to have inclusive language to include all of us. So I have attempted to be true to documenting the sources of every scriptural reference, using the New International Version translation for most of my references. However, this version is not wholly inclusive in its language. Therefore, I pray you will be indulgent as you read your select version and find it does not say "exactly" what I have stated. It's what I saw and felt was intended!

LICENSE

FREE TO THE READER OF THIS BOOK!

This license entitles the reader to weep, wail, sob, scream, moan, groan, and cry as you see fit!

The work of forgiveness is a journey through pain.

Tears are needed, expected, and required.

Use this license frequently!

Taking Back My Yesterdays

I am no longer innocent,
but I am not guilty of the wrong
you have done to me.
The sacred shadows of yesterday
rise like specters of injustice.

Like Banshee, they sound an alarm
meant to cower me,
but I will not.
Cower as others may,
I am not captive to your forever-sins,
neither victim of your momentary whims.

I am colorizing my memories,
sanctifying them for my future.
Stubbornness has taken hold of me,
and I am staring down the sorrow,
factoring in the pain,
and becoming Today and Tomorrow Strong.

The non-memories I have blocked,
I am filling with faith in a God
who moves forward and leads.

I want to take my medicine bag,
those healing stones
that helped me survive your cruelty.
I will need them
in the not-too-far successes
I will encounter.

You may not keep them.
And my tears are reserved
in a heavenly bottle numbered by Wisdom.
They belong to me again,
and are on account,
testifying against you.
No, you may no longer name yourself
my judge or my destiny.

All you stole, I now reclaim with force.
The violence you used against me—
that whirlwind that wrecked my life—
well, I have learned to harness winds and
    thunder.

The violence, I have turned to my own power.
And yes, I am here to take everything you kept:
pieces of my soul,
parts of my heart.
And my destiny.

The future is ahead, and I need them.
I am taking back my yesterdays.

VALERIE J. BRIDGEMAN DAVIS

1
A NEW LOOK AT YESTERDAY

And I am staring down the sorrow,
factoring in the pain,
and becoming Today and Tomorrow
    Strong.

             VALERIE J. BRIDGEMAN DAVIS

Father, forgive them, for they know
not what they do.

                  LUKE 23:34

PRINCIPLE

    WE NEED TO STEP BACK AND LOOK AT
    THE OTHER SIDE OF PAINFUL SITUA-
    TIONS. PUT SELF IN THEIR SHOES TO GET
    A DIFFERENT PERSPECTIVE.

I had no particular reason for my tears. By this, I mean that there was no plan on my part to work toward crying over my father. There had never been a conscious thought in my mind saying, "You need to shed tears and absolve him." Had this thought entered my mind, knowing myself as I do, it would have been immediately dismissed.

But one day the tears came.

I was sitting, reflecting upon my own life, feeling down, and wanting to have a pity party, and the tears began to flow freely. But they were not for me, the poor victim. These tears were for him, the poor victimizer!

I cried for the loss of his childhood. His mother died and his father "got lost" before he was seven years old. He didn't get to develop that necessary sense of security. His world was not a safe place where for just a little while he was the center of their universe. I cried for him. He needed my tears.

I cried for him having to fend for himself. His mother's two sisters lived together. One was married to an alcoholic and had five children of her own. The other was single, but she had already accepted responsibility for yet another sister's three sons. In this huge extended and dysfunctional family, my father tried to find a place to be somebody. No parents, no siblings, no one to watch his back. I cried for him. He needed my tears.

I cried for the dark color of his skin and the searching brilliance of his sharp mind. The schools should have been a safe place, but he was too dark. Black was not beautiful. To the world his dark skin equaled inferiority and lack of ability to think or articulate. The schools should have been a challenging and instructive place where his creative potential was appreciated and honored. This did not happen. I cried for him. He needed my tears.

I cried for the lack of affirmative action and equal opportunity, which imprisoned him in a laborer's job at the steel mills for thirty-five years. He had hopes and dreams. He wanted to climb and succeed. He wanted to contribute and be recognized. But the nation was too closed. That made the world too small. I cried for him. He needed my tears.

I didn't plan for the tears to come. I wasn't prepared for their intensity. But I cried for him. He needed my tears.

Did the tears absolve his sins toward me? Of course not! Did the tears wipe away the horrible memories and the pain of incest? Indeed not! Did the tears heal my wounded spirit and mend my broken heart? Not quite. But it was the beginning of my *taking back my yesterdays!*

The tears begin to melt the hate which had
gathered for too long around my heart. The
tears begin to wash my mind of the aged unforgiveness. The tears helped me to view the other
side of my father's story.

He was dead and had been for over twelve
years. But he needed my tears. And I cried for
him.

Rizpah

Holding my tears keeps me bound
Enslaves me to the pain.
Holding my tears straps the bitterness to
my back, binds the anger in my heart,
and I am becoming something different,
unrecognizable even to myself.
My joints once smooth and lubricated,
creak and swell. My head once elegantly
balanced, bows and sways and droops.
My heart once joyful and melodious,

skips beats and drops rhythms. My
bowels lock up and my blood ceases to
flow. Stop crying?

In a dry and weary land water is a
premium. In a dry and weary heart,
bitterness is tightly held. I present the
waters of my soul as an offering of who
I once was. Don't stop crying!

DEBORAH TINSLEY TAYLOR

PRAYER

Weeping God, thank you for another witness who understands the volume of my tears. I have often been ashamed of the many tears I have shed over my pain. But what else could I have done with this rip in my heart and gaping hole in my spirit? Thank you for giving me tears to release my pent-up screams, my held-in rage, and my overwhelming anger at yesterday. I can't see crying for this person who has hurt me so. My tears are for myself and for what was done to me. But I am willing to allow you to begin the work of transforming my life, for I want to take back my yesterdays. I submit my tears for you to use for my good. You alone are more than enough to handle every yesterday. Now, as I ask you to forgive me for my sin against you, please listen to the many good reasons I have for holding on to my unforgiveness at this one who has hurt me so.

PSALM 130

From the depths I call to you, Yahweh,

Lord, listen to my cry for help!

Listen compassionately to my pleading.

If you never overlooked our sins, Yahweh,

Lord, could anyone survive?

But, you do forgive us: and for that we
        revere you.

I wait for Yahweh, my soul waits.

I rely on Yahweh's promises,

my soul relies on the Lord more than a
        watchman on the coming of dawn.

Let Israel rely on Yahweh. . . .

For it is with Yahweh that mercy is to be
        found,

and a generous redemption;

it is Yahweh who redeems Israel

for all their sins.

ADAPTED FROM THE
JERUSALEM BIBLE

The psalmist knows the journey of tears and is experiencing isolation and alienation. Anguish has wrung a plea of extreme desperation from the lips of the psalmist, who understands our pain. And, like you, the author is waiting on God. Rewrite this psalm in your own words.

Principle

WE NEED TO STEP BACK AND LOOK AT
THE OTHER SIDE OF THE PAINFUL SITUA-
TION. FOR A FEW MINUTES TRY TO PUT
YOURSELF IN "THEIR" PLACE! THIS WILL
ALLOW YOU TO GET A DIFFERENT PER-
SPECTIVE. "FATHER, FORGIVE THEM, FOR
THEY KNOW NOT WHAT THEY DO!"
(LUKE 23:34).

The Jesus prayer from the cross is a reframing of
the situation he was undergoing. He had the
ability to step back and to look at the other side
of his pain. He understood that they were act-
ing in ignorance. The Roman officials felt they
were doing something to Jesus! Jesus understood that they were in need of something from
him! The same is true today. The one who hurt
you is in need of something from you. You have
this same ability as Jesus. The opportunity lies

before you. As you shatter the frame on the picture of yesterday and turn the picture to get another point of view, the photo will not change, but you will!

Consider

What could the person who hurt you possibly have needed from you?

Can you cry for another's pain and yet hold on to unforgiveness?

Tears are a gift which wash the windows of our souls and allow us to see more clearly. Can you offer the gift of tears for the one who needs your forgiveness?

When you stop crying for yourself and the pain of yesterday, what will you do with that energy?

Who will you be after you take back your yesterdays?

WEEK'S REFLECTIVE REVIEW

What has the Spirit of Life spoken to me this week?

This week I have chosen to do at least one thing differently. What is the Spirit of Life calling me to do?

What has the Spirit of Life taught me this week?

What are my goals for next week's gift of life?

What has the Spirit of Life inspired me to try?

What accomplishments do I celebrate this week?

Many instances and people have been blessings to my life this week. What am I especially grateful for?

CLOSING PRAYER

God of Yesterday, Today, and Tomorrow, I have spent seven whole days wrestling with my tears of pain. You discern my longing to be made whole. Help me as I continue the journey. Thank you for your unfailing love. May it be so, now and always. Amen.

2
FACING THE DEMONS, CONFRONTING THE TRUTH

I am no longer innocent,
but I am not guilty of the wrong
you have done to me.
The sacred shadows of yesterday
rise like specters of injustice.
Like Banshee, they sound an alarm
meant to cower me.

VALERIE J. BRIDGEMAN DAVIS

When you walk through the waters
I will be with you, and when you
walk through the fire, you shall not
be burned.

ISAIAH 43:2

Principle

> To forgive does not mean that you
> will ever forget! Remembering is
> confronting the harsh reality,
> facing the demonic, and knowing
> that God is with you to carry you
> through.

Life is often like a long journey. Sometimes the stretch ahead seems endless, dreary, and unexciting. Two hours had passed, and the journey still seemed to hold unrelenting distance. As Michigan gave away to Indiana, the green turned into more bleak browns and flatlands. For what seemed like miles, the scenery was simply blah. The sign indicated that the Indiana Dunes were up ahead. Memories of good times begin to dance and play.

A family picnic had been held there many years ago. Parents had a reunion with children and grandchildren in the picnic area of the dunes. Some traveled this very highway to be there. One came home from college, bringing a wife and new son. Hamburgers, hotdogs, and ribs simmered over the grills. Volleyball, horseshoes, and plain chitchat filled the air with excitement and the joy of good times. It was an echo of family at its best. It brought a smile.

"No!" shouted the voice in my head. "If you remember this incident as 'good,' you will forget what he did to you!" I can, even now, remember the jerk of my head as I tried to shake the memories and return to my reality, which was filled with anger, pain, and unforgiveness.

We had been raised with the understanding that you "forgive and forget." It seemed reasonable that if I could remember something good, then I must be forgetting what he had done in the past. If I forgave him, wouldn't that mean I condoned his actions? How could my mind try to trick me into believing that my family could have ever had "good" times when my father had been so horrible? Determination came to stand tall in my conscious mind. "Linda, you cannot forgive what he did, and you will never forget!"

The Bible lists the word "forgive" a total of fifty-three times. (Of course, if you count "forgiveness," "forgiven," and "forgiving," you will find more!) The very first time the word is used, we find the brothers of Joseph, who had put him in a pit and sold him into slavery, asking forgiveness. Their father, Israel, had died. Knowing what they had done and the years of separation they had forced upon their brother, they felt he would be justified in holding a grudge against them. So they sent a message to Joseph telling him that this was the request and instruction of their father. " 'I ask you to forgive your brothers the sins and the wrongs they committed in treating you so badly. Now please forgive the sins of the servants of the God of your father.' When their message came to him, Joseph wept" (Genesis 50:17).

These siblings knew they had sinned and done wrong. There was no question in their minds that they had earned revenge and payback for the evils they had committed. They had decided to kill him twenty years earlier, then recanted and simply sold him off into slavery. They had denied him access to his family. They had stolen years of being nurtured by his father. Then they had lived a lie and kept their father's heart in grief for all of those years. Surely they were afraid of payback! Of course they thought he would be out to get them now that their father was dead. Yet they sought forgiveness.

They did not ask forgiveness on the ground that they deserved it. They already knew what they deserved for the wrongs they had committed. Had the tables been turned and one of them been in Joseph's shoes, they knew what sort of harsh judgement they would have meted out! But the value they pointed to was their father and their father's God. Forgive for a higher purpose. Forgive because we are family.

Forgive because God constantly forgives us. Without the word "forgive" there is no Christian religion. Without the word "forgive" there would have been no need for God to send Jesus. Without the word "forgive" we could not be in relationship with our God. We have been forgiven in the past and continually need forgiveness today! And yet we find it so difficult to forgive.

Webster's New Collegiate Dictionary defines the word "forgive" in this manner: 1) to cease to feel resentment against an offender: to pardon one's enemies; 2) to give up claim to requital for an insult; to grant relief from payment of a debt; to excuse. The synonyms include: utilize, overlook, absolve, excuse, acquit, liberate, discharge, deliver, and free. All of these are interesting words which put the ball in our court!

We have to be willing to give up our claim to hold on to the past. We have to be generous enough to grant to another liberation from any payment. It is within our power to exonerate, clear, and wipe clean the slate of someone who has hurt us. This is just what Jesus came to do for us! Can we be like Jesus toward others?

When you try to see what this feels like and looks like, imagine taking a bat and smashing, breaking, and beating into a million pieces the unrealistic picture you had in mind of yesterday. For all of *Webster's* definitions point toward facing the reality that people will do stupid and hurtful things. We have to be bigger than those who do these acts toward us. To for-give is to let go of any and all make-believe concepts and fantasies which cause us to see them coming to us sorry, contrite, crying, and falling on their knees, begging our forgiveness!

Would you believe that the first time the word "forgive" is used in the New Testament is when Jesus teaches the disciples to pray? "Forgive us our debts, as we forgive those who trespass against us" (Matthew 6:12). When we will not forgive and let go of what others have done to us, we cannot expect forgiveness for our own sins! This says nothing about forget-ting, my friend. But we are held responsible to forgive.

You cannot forget! You cannot forget because the mind is more sophisticated and complex than the most advanced computer. In fact, computers are facsimiles of the human mind. We have memory, and it is a gift. Memory helps us learn to talk, to add, and to recall facts. Memory keeps present with us the loved ones who have died. Memory assists us by not allowing those who have hurt us in the past to again take the center stage in our life. This life is a video of your own making. Everybody does not deserve a starring role. Some folks are bit players; some are walk-on characters who show up and then disappear; everybody does not get equal billing in your life.

Some wise person said that if you forget the past, you are bound to repeat it. I don't want to forget what my father did to me. Joseph did not ever say that he would forget what his brothers had done. This is what he told them: "You intended to harm me, but God intended it for good to accomplish what is now being done" (Genesis 50:19). He announced his own benediction and dismissed himself from their turmoil! He refused to get trapped in the game of one-upmanship which could have been expected after twenty years of feeling abandoned, rejected, and hurt. Joseph said goodbye, farewell, adios to those common human feelings of being resentful and begrudging. In this instance, he gave God the credit for his life and was able to see the larger picture. It does not mean that their roles in putting him in a pit in the first place were minimized. It does not mean that he enjoyed the suffering they inflicted as they made fun of his dreams and hated him for no just cause. But it meant that God took the bad and made good use of it in him. And, in retrospect, he was able to see the hand of God at work in his "yesterday"!

I will never forget my past. Today I can remember the dunes picnic with a lasting smile. It was a good time. I enjoyed my family that day. It was good to have been in the company of my father and mother, sisters and brothers in that particular instance. And I remember the pain of the incest and family denial. However, I can now see how God has taken it and integrated it into a larger life, a bigger picture.

My writing, preaching, teaching, and living have grown out of my remembering the pain. My life is more than the pain my father inflicted. Like Joseph, I know God has a plan for my life which is larger than the pit of incest! Life is a long journey, and one stop along the way is not the entire trip!

Womanrising

Is there a guide for me?
Am I lost? Am I weak?
In the midst of the day I
call out to you
In the midst of the night
I look within the center of my being
in the silences

Where is my strength?
It comes in the remembrances
I am a daughter of Isis
Sister of Joseph
Mother of Time
Though my flesh be torn and sheared
from my bone
Though my spirit be stripped and blown
about the ages like cosmic lint
I shall endure!

When tomorrow comes
I will walk into it with my head up
Trustful, sure, upright and courageous
Praise God, oh my soul.

DEBORAH TINSLEY TAYLOR

PRAYER

Caring, Comforting, and Compassionate God, how long have I tried not to remember yesterday? You know the many and varied ways and methods I have used to try and avoid this painful reality. Now the Truth comes declaring that I will never forget! Help me walk through these memories. Carry me over the wide chasms of despair. Bear me up as the weight of sorrow tries to overwhelm and pull me back into the depths of depression and hopelessness. Prop me up when I feel that I am about to drown in the sea of pain. Forgive me for forgetting that you have promised to never leave me alone! Be with me now, as I remember those moments of pain.

PSALM 51

> Have mercy on me, O God, in your
>   goodness,
> in your great tenderness wipe away my
>   faults;
> wash me clean of my guilt,
> purify me from my sin.
> For I am well aware of my faults,
> I have my sin constantly in mind,
> having sinned against none other than
>   you,
> having done what you regard as wrong.
> Yet, since you love sincerity of heart,
> teach me the secrets of wisdom. . . .
> Instill some joy and gladness into me. . . .
> Let my crushed bones rejoice again. . . .
> God, create a clean heart in me, put into me
> a new and constant spirit.
> Do not banish me from your presence,
> do not deprive me of your Holy Spirit.

Be my Savior again, renew my joy,

keep my spirit steady and willing. . . .

ADAPTED FROM THE

JERUSALEM BIBLE

As David remembered and wrote down his request, remember and request of God now.

PRINCIPLE

> TO FORGIVE DOES NOT MEAN THAT YOU
> WILL EVER FORGET! REMEMBERING IS
> CONFRONTING THE HARSH REALITY,
> FACING THE DEMONIC, AND KNOWING
> THAT GOD IS WITH YOU TO CARRY YOU
> THROUGH! "WHEN YOU PASS THROUGH
> THE WATERS, I WILL BE WITH YOU, AND
> WHEN YOU WALK THROUGH THE FIRE,
> YOU SHALL NOT BE BURNED" (ISAIAH
> 43:2).

There are many lies we have been taught about
forgiveness. Among them are: "To forgive
means you have to forget," "If I forgive this it
will happen again," "If I forgive this it means
that I condone it." The real truth is that you
cannot, should not, and most likely will not
ever forget! It's time to debunk these myths
which keep us stuck in yesterday. It's time to

face the reality that "forgiving and forgetting" does not work! Why would you want to forget?

CONSIDER

"Then Peter came to Jesus and asked, 'Lord, how
many times shall I forgive my siblings when
they sin against me? Up to seven times?' Jesus
answered, 'I tell you, not seven times, but sev-
enty-seven times!' " (Matthew 18:21–22). We
are promised a life span of approximately sev-
enty years. There are seven days in every
week. Could this possibly mean that every
day of our lives we are responsible to forgive
our siblings because we are family?

Have you ever dared sing "Come and go with me
to my father's house, there will be peace,
peace, peace"? What does this song say to
you about forgiveness among the people of
God?

Is it possible to see your yesterday in a different context than your pain? In other words, how would this incident seem if it had happened to the person you don't want to forgive?

Within you lies the capacity to forgive! For planted within you lie the capabilities of greatness and success. This is another day of choice for you. Don't allow the past to scare you, paralyze your growth, and keep you stuck in yesterday. We have a history of surviving, living, and thriving. We did it because of our determination, perseverance, and dependence on the Spirit of New Beginnings. Listen to what the Spirit has to say to you now.

WEEK'S REFLECTIVE REVIEW
What has the Spirit of Life spoken to me this
    week?

This week I have chosen to do at least one thing
    differently. What is the Spirit of Life calling
    me to do?

What has the Spirit of Life taught me this week?

What are my goals for next week's gift of life?

What has the Spirit of Life inspired me to try?

What accomplishments do I celebrate this week?

Many instances and people have been blessings in
    my life this week. What am I especially grate-
    ful for?

CLOSING PRAYER

God of Grace and God of Glory, thank you for helping me to know that one bad trip is not the whole of my journey! Thank you for your Amazing Grace which continues to sustain me along the way! May it be so now and always.

3
TAKING BACK MY STUFF

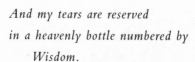

*And my tears are reserved
in a heavenly bottle numbered by
Wisdom.*

VALERIE J. BRIDGEMAN DAVIS

*Record my lament, capture my tears
in your bottle.*

PSALM 56:8

PRINCIPLE

WITH PRECISION AND DELIBERATE
EFFORT THE GRIEVING FOR YESTERDAY
MUST BE ENCOUNTERED. IT'S ALL RIGHT
TO CRY AND LAMENT.

The session had begun when I entered. I quickly found a seat and tried to "catch up" with the speaker. As I looked around there were several familiar faces in the large crowd. When the speaker finished and instructions were given for the afternoon, we prepared to move on to the next place. From behind me came the sound of my name. It was the husband of my former best friend! He kissed my cheek, we made social chitchat, and we left the room.

Busily engaged in trying to find the assigned room, I didn't see *her* standing at the top of the stairs. Once again I heard my name, and as I looked up, surprise and shock rose to meet me. It was *her.* We had not seen each other in four years, since the day that she had told me, "I no longer want to be your best friend, I need my space!" Much more than distance had separated us. And here she was in my world.

She came forward to embrace me. I stood there. Like a statue, I could not move to return the hug. The questions were swirling in my head, my mind was filled with confusion, and I really didn't know what to do, what to say, or how to act. So, I stood there. Here we were, two of the most talkative people in the world, surrounded by silence. Finally she stepped back and asked, "What room are you looking for?" She directed me to the room and I went inside, feeling as perplexed as could be.

The fog of the unknown had camped around me. The old anger was rising. And confusion reigned supreme. I had learned how to live without her in my life! I had determined never to trust another female friend with my innermost thoughts after we had parted almost four years before. Our relationship had been so tight, so close and so interwoven, that the repercussion of our falling out was known across the

country! We had been closer than most biological sisters. Her mother had adopted me, for my
mother was dead. Her sister was my sister and
my sisters accepted and acknowledged her place
in my life. Both of our spouses were well accustomed to our twice-a-day, sometimes hour-
long phone conversations. If one was in a meet-
ing, part of a conference, or hosting a special
gathering, you could believe that the other one
would be there as chief cheerleader! Then came
the death of our relationship. The grief was
numbing. The pain was intense. The embarrass-
ment was overwhelming as I tried to explain
away her absence in my life.

I sat there for over an hour as the noted
speaker addressed the group. A racing dialogue
carried on inwardly. Why did she have to be
here? Why didn't I know she was going to be
here? Why hadn't her husband told me that she
was here? Why in the world did she come and

hug me like we had parted recently, in friendship? Who in this gathering knows about our
former close friendship?

When the session was finally over, I hur-
ried back to my room to call my husband. I felt
like a little, confused child. The adult in me had
retreated and the hurt and angry child was
demanding attention. "Lynn, you can handle
this," my husband gently chided. "There is no
place and no reason for you to hide." I lay in my
room and allowed my mind to replay our relationship. She had meant so much to me. We had
shared so much with one another. We were soul
sisters. Then she had pulled away. My hurt and
anger were intense. The feelings were the type
that lingered.

Now here she was again, in my life, on my
stage and in my world. Did yesterday have the
ability to dictate my today? I had planned for
and looked forward to this event; would I dare

allow her to ruin it for me? I realized that in reacting to her presence, I was putting my power at her disposal. Once again I was replaying the scene of the poor, needy sister. Well, I had grown. I had learned some new lessons. I had moved from that old space. And my "today" would not be stolen! As a matter of fact, I was ready to go, encounter her, and take back my yesterday!

With precision and deliberate effort, I got up and dressed with care. Then I set out to find "Sista." As I recall my emotions, there was no fighting anger within me. I wanted resolution. And I needed some answers about "yesterday." When I found her, there was an expected cold front. Yet I engaged her to set aside some time for food and discussion. The ball was in my court and I was determined to play this set to the finish.

Conflict resolution is not a familiar concept to most women. We know how to get angry and run away, or to stay and engage in fights which no one wins, or we learn how to sulk and to hope that someone will pay attention and allow us to have our way. But to find an answer and put the matter to rest requires hard work and emotional energy. This was the timing of the Holy Spirit, for both of us were in the same place. It was time to get down to business.

The ministry of reconciliation belongs to the people of God. How often I had forgotten this fact in the days gone by. I wallowed in my grief. I allowed my anger and hurt to escalate. And I was determined to find some way to hurt her as badly as I had been hurt. Yes, I was saved, born again, and Spirit-filled! Yes, I wrote books, preached, and taught about inner healing! But the enemy of our souls cares not about our credentials. The plan had been to deceive me into thinking that yesterday held the most secure power over me. But I realized that I was not the

same woman today that I had been yesterday!
Time, growth, maturity, and much inner reflection belonged to me. Yes, for a minute I had
regressed and lost it! But I didn't regress com-
pletely into yesterday's behavior.

We arranged time at breakfast and she
came just before it was over. I didn't get defen-
sive or angry. I realized that her tardiness was a
cover for her own nervousness and fear. So, gra-
ciously, I suggested that perhaps we could talk
between sessions and agreed to meet in an open
but quiet spot.

"I need to know what caused you to pull
away from our relationship." There was no
blame in my statement. There were no recrim-
inations and there was no anger. I simply had a
need for information that only she could sup-
ply. The conversation lasted almost two hours
as we shared back and forth and discovered
new truths about each other and about our-

selves. We caught up on family matters and the children. We talked about our husbands. And we both confessed to the sad and empty space within us. Our tears ran for the relationship that had been and was now over. My anger was gone. My sadness was lessened. I recognized that we had moved to closure of our relationship. We had celebrated and buried a former "friend." We could move on. I was at peace.

Another sista friend, Daisy Thomas-Quinney, a pretty sharp woman, told me that "friends are given to us for seasons and for reasons." Not all friends come into our lives to stay. Some come and bring new things. Some come and take whatever they can. Some come to go part of life's journey with us. And some come to touch your life with love. But friends don't come to stay at the same level and in the same function forever. As much as we would love to "freeze frame" certain relationships and hold them in storage forever, life moves on. For each of us grows, matures, and progresses in life. But we can each learn some new lessons from others. Some different flavors and distinct characteristics are added to our life by the rich variety of our friends. And at times, some pain and hurt are stirred into the friendship. For friends are intimate associates. Friends can get so close that we forget we are separate and distinct individuals. So, along comes change!

Tears

These tears are for me
I cried so hard
I thought a faucet had been left on
to flow through my eyes
I couldn't see.
I cried for all the times I couldn't
When I was made to shut up
And not allowed to feel the

unspeakable and the unnameable
The horrific that assailed and
assaulted my mind and body
and those whom I loved.

These tears are for you
I cried so hard
I thought the tides had risen and
the oceans flooded through my eyes
I cried because you couldn't. . . .

These tears are for all of us.
I cried so hard
I thought the sky had broke open
and rain ran from my eyes in torrents
I couldn't see
I cried for all the times
we couldn't
because we were made to shut up. . . .

DEBORAH TINSLEY TAYLOR

PRAYER

Friend of the Friendless, you know the pain of
betrayal and rejection by friends. The anguish is
soul-deep and grievous to the tender spirit. The
loss of a good friend is like death. I have grieved.
I have mourned. I have felt alone. In my hurt I
could not forgive. I wanted to hide the depth of
my distress. I tried to act as if I did not really care
that a piece of me was missing! I acted a lie. I was
the great pretender. For I wondered what was
wrong with me, what I had done to cause this
rift. My heart felt as if it were breaking. My tears
spoke what my lips refused to say. Now forgiveness is knocking at my door. Can I do this? Can
I release the shame and humiliation I was caused?
Do I really want to cancel out all my plans for
getting revenge and justification for my hurt
feelings? When all of your friends ran off and left
you to face death alone, how did you forgive
them? Speak to my waiting heart!

PSALM 133

How good it is, how pleasant,
for [sisters] to live in unity.
It is like the precious oil
running down from Aaron's head and beard,
down to the collar of his robes.
It is like the dew on Mount Hermon
falling on the hills of Zion.
For there Yahweh has promised a blessing,
life that never ends.

FROM PSALMS ANEW

Relationships are precious and unity is desired by God. When there is harmony in friendships, we are renewed and revitalized! When there is a rupture, life seems to ebb away. Who has caused you to shed the most tears recently due to a broken relationship? Can you face them now?

PRINCIPLE

> WITH PRECISION AND DELIBERATE
> EFFORT THE GRIEVING FOR YESTERDAY
> MUST BE ENCOUNTERED. IT'S ALL RIGHT
> AND IT'S PROPER TO CRY AND TO
> LAMENT. "RECORD MY LAMENT, CAP-
> TURE MY TEARS IN YOUR BOTTLE"
> (PSALM 56:8).

When we change, so does our destiny! The life we have planned to simply endure, we now learn to engage and enjoy. When you decide to stand up from a bent-over position, there are major decisions to be made. When your eyes become open to what you have allowed someone else to keep from you, it's with precision and force that you strategize your next move. You will discover that every day is a new day where you can recognize the "old" you in the face and actions of another! Gratitude begins as you ascertain just how far you have moved from that position. How are you different today than yesterday?

CONSIDER

What needs to be done to bring closure to the
    relationship that has caused you so much
    pain? If the relationship was a pie, cut in eight
    pieces, how many pieces are actual pain?
    How many pieces are shame and humilia-
    tion? How many pieces are your need and
    desire for revenge and payback? How many
    pieces are your anger that this was done to
    you?

Draw the pie. Look at your true feelings.

Write a letter to the one who hurt you. Act as if
    it is a face-to-face encounter. Be honest. For
    the matter needs to be aired. Then grace can
    help you with the issue of restoration. Re-
    conciliation is awaiting your move. Just do it!

Who have you hurt in a similar manner? What
relationship did you just drop without explanation? What steps do you need to take as
you face your own actions?

WEEK'S REFLECTIVE REVIEW

What has the Spirit of Life spoken to me this week?

This week I have chosen to do at least one thing differently. What is the Spirit of Life calling me to do?

What has the Spirit of Life taught me this week?

What are my goals for next week's gift of life?

What has the Spirit of Life inspired me to try?

What accomplishments do I celebrate this week?

Many instances and people have been blessings to my life this week. What am I especially grateful for?

CLOSING PRAYER

Companion on My Journey, thank you for never going away and turning your back on me. There has never been a time that you have not been a faithful friend. I have been so focused on how my former friend hurt me that I neglected to remember that I have not always been a loyal friend! Thank you for going with me down memory lane. Thank you for Grace who has enveloped each step. May it be so now and always.

4
SELF-ABSOLUTION

*No, you may no longer name yourself
my judge or my destiny.*

VALERIE J. BRIDGEMAN DAVIS

*Stand at the crossroads and look, ask
for the ancient paths, ask where the
good way is and walk in it, and
you shall find rest for your soul.*

JEREMIAH 6:16

PRINCIPLE

REALIZE THAT YOU MAKE YOUR OWN
DAY! YOUR SOUL IS YOUR ONLY POSSES-
SION. OTHERS DO NOT HAVE THE
POWER TO KEEP YOUR SOUL!

I met her at church one Sunday morning. She was young, beautiful, and filled with rage. After worship she said she needed to talk with me. But the call never came. So I called her. We talked of the constant pain she carried. We talked about her being abandoned, over and over again. Her mother, a single woman, had left her to be raised by her grandmother. When Grandmother died she felt the rejection demon surface again. So we talked about her heart becoming hard and her trust level around every relationship being a minus ten. We talked about how she needed to talk, to grieve the many mini-deaths of her life, to journey through her pain and take back her yesterdays.

She joined the women's support group. Really she made the support group happen. She made the phone calls. She worked to establish an agenda. She bought and served refreshments. She was the chief cheerleader for every sister involved. She listened and she talked.

We adopted each other. I became Rev. Mom and she became my daughter. We kept working on her issues. When she tried to back up as the pain became more intense, the group pushed her and I encouraged her to hold on. When she had to kick, scream, rant, and rave, I listened and told her that wholeness was worth the effort. When she needed to argue, I argued with her. When she needed to cry, we cried together. For two years we struggled as she fought to take back her yesterdays. In the midst of her growth, her birth mother was found dead. She was responsible for her mother's funeral. For the next year she wrestled with her pain, determined to take back her soul. Listen as she reveals her own story, lifted from the pages of her journal.

To my daughter
To my mother
A letter from the grave

                              BY JACQUI FORD

I guess that I've known for a long time
now that I would have to confront the
demons of my past and my relationship
with you, my daughter. I just never
thought that I would have to confront
them from the grave. So I'll start first by
saying that I love you and have always
loved you. I'm sorry that you didn't
know it sooner and that it took
death—oh how death makes you grieve
your life choices—for me to tell you so.
I've always wanted you. But the pain
that was in my heart and my over-
whelming need to find happiness didn't
allow me to rejoice in your birth.

*You are the woman from whose womb I was
conceived. I was conceived out of passion, not
out of love. Growing in your womb but not
in your heart, I was given no beginning, no
middle, and no end. You see, you gave me
life, but you could not give me "me"! Now
death makes it impossible to recapture lost
years' time. My mother—what did you
allow our lives to become?*

My daughter, how I grieve and have
grieved our lost years together. Looking
back now, I remember when the doctor
placed you in my arms and I looked
into your round chubby little face. I
looked into a face that was looking
back at me with such love. I cried that
day for the life I knew you were des-
tined to have—a life of sorrow, hurt,
and pain brought on by the errors of

my life and your father's life. Our self-
ishness and lack of love would and did
become your nightmare.

*I look in the mirror and I see a resemblance
of you. Your daughter whose eyes could not
sparkle like the rare diamonds that they are
because of the veil of sorrow that glazes over
them. I see a smile that could not glisten
with a ray of sunshine, because it has been
overcast with sadness. My mother, what have
you done to me?*

My child, even from the grave I feel
your hurt. Your unanswered questions,
your unasked questions have weighed
heavy on my heart. How I hope that
you will find the answers you search for
and need so that you can find peace
from this mess I've created with our

lives. I wish that I could change things—but death only allows room for reflection. So I give you this letter, this explanation in the hopes that you will find inner happiness and tranquility from my mistakes.

Mother, you took my soul when you took my history. My dreams go unfulfilled, my hopes unknown. And my love for my mother has been an open wound. I was not left with a memory to bury or a cherished moment to comfort my soul. So, a memory of what you are, what you were, and what you could have been is left to linger in the subregions of my mind, my thoughts, and my heart. All because you were the mother that I did not know.

My daughter—I had dreams. I dreamed that my life would have been different from what it was. But now that seems like an eternity ago. How I wanted just a taste of the life that was portrayed in the many books that I liked to read. I wanted to feel the love, experience the romance, travel the world to far-away and exotic places and sample the adventure that all of that could bring. It's sad, but I had to settle for a life so far away from the life that I had envisioned. So . . . I lived the only life that I knew how. Yes, I lived fifty-one years of brokenness and loneliness. Always despondent over the events that had shaped my life. It became my armor of protection until my heart could not bear the weight of it all and simply stopped beating.

In search for the happiness, I neglected what meant the most to me.

Only to realize that years had passed
and then it was too late to recapture
what I had lost—you. Or . . . maybe I
did not want it back. Because to get it
back would mean that I would have
had to face the demons of what I had
done to someone I had carried under
my bosom for nine months. I would
have to face myself and the fact that I
did not know your favorite color,
favorite food, what made you smile, or
what made you sad. I would have had
to realize that I did not know what
your dreams were. And, sadly . . . you
did not know mine.

So I accepted the physical abuse,
the mental anguish, and the turbulent
emotional roller coaster ride the men in
my life inflicted upon me—this willing
victim. I thought that was what life had

in store for me and maybe this was really love. Only it wasn't, and alcoholism became my escape into the fantasy world that I had longed for.

Love can be one-sided sometimes. And it sure can hurt most of the time. Never love anything or anybody more than you love yourself. But then you are a strong young woman—not like me. I wasn't strong enough to handle your father's rejection, so I internalized the hurt and rejection. I guess you can say that it only made me feel as if I wasn't worthy of love and happiness. So when I was given up on—I gave in and gave up on loving that which was left of our moments together.

Accept this not as an excuse, but as truth. So I searched . . . hoping to find true love and happiness. Now . . . six feet under the moist earth, I have realized that I could have felt some love if only I had taken the time to look into the eyes and bathe in the love that radiated from the heart of the child who resembled what I had lost.

You left me, your child, to fly on her own—wounded, hurt, and alone. We should have been two hearts, governed and sanctioned by the bond of mother-daughter love. For you see it was you that gave me life and you could have given me a history. Now all that is left is the shared bloodline that runs through my veins.

I apologize for all that I was and all that I wasn't. I now give thanks that you had someone to love you, to protect you, and to care for you when I didn't and

couldn't. So please do not replay or
rehash the past. Lay to rest those feelings of hurt and anger at the things that
I did and did not do. For you see, I
now hurt enough for both of us. Oh
how death gives one time for reflecting!

So my daughter, please find some
good in my life and some lessons in my
living. There were some of each. If you
can, find forgiveness in your heart so
that you can find inner healing and
peace from the mess that I've made of
our lives. You see, I want you to live in
happiness and wholeness, that which I
never could.

A part of my soul will always ache for you,
because you are the first woman I ever knew.
I will always shed tears of remorse for you,
because you are the one that gave me my

*beginning on this earth. I am saddened that
death had to pay a visit before you made
peace with yourself and with me. But, then,
only with death can the soul rejoice in the
peace and tranquility of life's dilemmas. So I
say to you—"You are forgiven. You were
always loved. And you are loved."*

Now my spirit can finally rest peaceful-
ly. Thank you for your forgiveness. I
love you!

MAMA

Girlfriend came to the point of forgiving her
mother after her death. But, most importantly,
she came to the place where she forgave herself!
How difficult it is to let go of the anger, guilt,
and hostility which builds within us. "What did
I do/not do that has caused others to treat me
in this way?" This question, in many different

forms, rises up to haunt us as we live with our pain. We must come to comprehend that life is not fair! Folks don't always make the best choices for the outcomes of their lives or ours! And it's not a matter of what we did or did not do that we must concern ourselves with all of our lives. The issue is that we must discern what life is trying to teach us!

In going through these very painful discussions Jacqui learned several lessons about herself and her biological mother. She learned that her mother was a woman of flesh and blood who had her own needs and desires. She learned that her mother had hurt, suffered, and experienced pain and rejection in her life. She learned that her mother did not know how to snatch back her yesterday!

Jacqui's self-awareness was heightened as she acknowledged that she had always loved, longed for, and needed her mother. She came to understand that women have always had to make choices that were difficult and complicated. She awakened to the reality that love all by its naked self is not enough to sustain relationships, even those between a mother and her baby daughter. Finally, she was able to release the unrealistic expectation of an awesome and emotional reconciliation. She came to accept her mother's limitations and her own.

The ties between women are closely linked. From the beginning we have had to choose our own destiny, not realizing how we were also binding others in the generations to come. Women have endured much wrongful blame and unnecessary guilt. Like Jacqui, some of us are learning how to release, relax, and let it go!

Muddy Black

I am Muddy Black

I am of the same beautiful black earth

the same crystal water and frosted

wind from which God fashioned the

first of all

I am Muddy Black

I am sacred

I am worthy

I am forever held within God

For God has made me and

I am Muddy Black

DEBORAH TINSLEY TAYLOR

PRAYER

Wisdom of Women, we are created in your image. You gifted us with sensitive and caring emotions. We carry so much of others inside ourselves. For too long I have hauled guilt for so much! I have guilt that is rightfully mine and that which belongs to others. In every rejection I have questioned my own "isness." I have wondered what was wrong with me, where my deficit was, what more I needed. I can now acknowledge that what I was doing was questioning and blaming you. Forgive my fault-finding with your divine design in me. Help me to fully acknowledge my sin, which is ever before me. And help me to lay aside everybody else's sin and guilt. Listen as I sort through "stuff" that is most likely not mine.

PSALM 90:1–2, 14–17

Lord, you have been our dwelling place in all
    generations.
Before the mountains were brought forth,
or ever you had formed the earth and the
    world.
From everlasting to everlasting you are God. . . .
Satisfy us in the morning with your steadfast
    love,
so that we may rejoice and be glad all our
    days.
Make us glad as many days as you have
    afflicted us,
and as many years as we have seen evil.
Let your work be manifest to your servants,
and your glorious power to their children.
Let the favor of the Lord our God be upon us,
and prosper for us the work of our hands—
O prosper the work of our hands!

                        ADAPTED FROM THE NRSV

PRINCIPLE

> REALIZE THAT YOU MAKE YOUR OWN
> DAY! YOUR SOUL IS YOUR ONLY POSSES-
> SION. OTHERS DO NOT HAVE THE
> POWER TO KEEP YOUR SOUL! "STAND AT
> THE CROSSROADS AND LOOK, ASK FOR
> THE ANCIENT PATHS, ASK WHERE THE
> GOOD WAY IS AND WALK IN IT, AND YOU
> SHALL FIND REST FOR YOUR SOUL"
> (JEREMIAH 6:16).

"Now I lay me down to sleep. I pray the Lord my soul to keep." This is one of the earliest prayers we learn. It is now time to realize that our souls do indeed belong to us! The soul is a possession we own and do not have to give over to the power of others. As we seek a safe environment and receive support from community for who we are, we can break the silence and shed the garments of shame and guilt that we have worn over our unforgivableness. This step begins to expand our worldview and allows us to forgive ourselves, absolve our guilt, and receive affirmation of who we are and can become. The actual risk is to go deep inside and to discover what wonderful women we really are! This is the initial step to self-absolution.

Name the wonderful things about you.

CONSIDER

Who have you given possession of your soul?

There is forgiveness available even for those on the other side of life! Like Jacqui, can you write a letter in both your voice and the voice of the individual you need to forgive? Or can you sit in a chair and have the other person face you in an empty chair? Talk aloud, then listen!

Jacqui's mother accepted physical abuse, mental anguish, and the turbulent emotional roller coaster ride the men in her life inflicted upon her as a willing victim. She did not view herself as worthy to demand or receive more from life. What do you need to demand from others for yourself now?

Abandonment is usually an issue for women. We
    tie ourselves to those who are really unwor-
    thy of our love because we do not want to be
    alone. Yet the question arises, who do you
    need to abandon in order to be whole?

WEEK'S REFLECTIVE REVIEW

What has the Spirit of Life spoken to me this
    week?

This week I have chosen to do at least one thing
    differently. What is the Spirit of Life calling
    me to do?

What has the Spirit of Life taught me this week?

What are my goals for next week's gift of life?

What has the Spirit of Life inspired me to try?

What accomplishments do I celebrate this week?

Many instances and people have been blessings to
    my life this week. What am I especially grate-
    ful for?

CLOSING PRAYER

Holy Memory, thank you for allowing me to go within and discover the treasures of myself! I am a worthwhile and worthy woman of value and significance. The load of shame and guilt is less today for you have helped me to dump garbage that was not mine. Let the lightness of my spirit and the flight of my soul carry me to others who need a sister-friend. I have been so blessed to discover hope for tomorrow and to even begin to see the promise you had placed in my yesterdays. May it be now and always.

5
HARNESSING WINDS AND THUNDER

The violence you used against me—
that whirlwind that wrecked my
> *life—*
well, I have learned to harness winds
> *and thunder.*
The violence, I have turned to my
> *own power.*

> VALERIE J. BRIDGEMAN DAVIS

This is what the Sovereign Lord
says, Come from the four winds,
O Breath, and breathe into these
dry bones that they may live.

> EZEKIEL 37:9

PRINCIPLE

> THE OLD, DESTRUCTIVE ANGER WHICH
> HELD YOU BACK WILL BE CONVERTED,
> TRANSFORMED, AND CHANGED INTO
> NEW HEALING ENERGY FOR YOURSELF
> AND FOR OTHERS.

It was the Sunday before Christmas. All was not well. The adult Sunday school class was studying from Maxie Dunham's *Workbook of Living Prayers.* As I prepared to bring the session to a close, I raised Maxie's question and instruction. "When was the last time you made a bold request of God? Make a bold prayer request now!"

I laughed. Then I prayed, "Lord, I want reconciliation with my daughter and grandson." Life went on. It was not well.

Our grandson, Giraurd Chase, had been brought to our home from the hospital. Most of his first four years had been spent in our home. He called me "Grand" and my husband, Chuck, "Pa-Pa," but primarily we were his parents. We had never assumed legal custody, but financial, educational, emotional, and spiritual responsibility we had willingly accepted.

How do I dress up the fact that my only daughter was involved with drugs? How do I make it sound nice that her lifestyle was not concerned with raising a child? How was I to resolve the matter of wanting her life to be different, better, changed while knowing the reality. We kept the child and allowed her to do her thing. This could be viewed as enabling. It could be viewed as rescuing the child. It could be viewed as the best option for an ugly situation.

I had given myself an elegant sit-down dinner for over fifty friends to celebrate my fiftieth birthday. Loved ones came from far and near to be present. Grian and the baby were conspicuously absent. But two days later she showed up to drop the baby off and never came back to reclaim him. Talk about resentment, anger, and unforgivingness. Both Chuck and I were enraged. We thought we had raised her to accept responsibility. We thought we had shown her enough love for her to want to pass it on. We thought it was finally our turn to live! But we were raising a grandson.

Two months before Thanksgiving Chuck and I made arrangements, in agreement with Giraurd's mother, to allow mutual friends to keep him while Chuck and I went on vacation. The first week that we were gone she "stole" him.

For two months we didn't see him or her. For two months we heard his voice only once. She had him leave a message on the answering machine which tore at our hearts. For two months it was agony just walking into his bedroom, looking at the Little Mermaid placemat on the kitchen table, or even calling his name. There is no describing our pain. There is no explaining our anger. I cannot begin to detail our growing resentment toward our daughter. There was no need to talk about forgiveness.

But I made a bold request of the Lord. We wanted to be involved in their life. We needed to know they were well, healthy, and safe. We wanted to see, touch, and talk to them. They are family. So I prayed for reconciliation. What would it look like? How would it occur? How would any of us act if reconciliation happened? Could we forgive her again?

My Monday began as usual with four clergy sisters gathered around my kitchen table studying scriptures for the next Sunday's sermon. Around 10:30 A.M. my phone rang. It was Giraud Chase! "Grand, is that you?" For fifteen precious minutes we talked, laughed, and questioned each other. "He wanted to talk to you," my daughter said before she disconnected the call. I had no phone number to call again, but my heart was singing.

Late that Thursday, just before choir rehearsal, I checked the voice mail. "Your daughter is in the hospital. Please call." Calling the nursing station, I asked the nurse to inquire whether we should pick up Giraurd from the sitter. The response was a firm "No." Pain again. Rejection. Anger. Hurt.

Chuck went home and I went into rehearsal as we prepared for the Christmas Eve worship service. Fifteen minutes later he was back at the church looking quizzical. "The babysitter called. She wants one of us to come and get Giraurd!"

I sat in the sanctuary listening as the choir practiced "I'll Be Home for Christmas." Just as they finished, the doors opened and down the aisle ran a screaming Giraurd. The choir went crazy. I sat and cried. That night I visited Grian in the hospital. She didn't know that we had Giraurd. We didn't touch or talk. I stood, looking down at my very pregnant daughter, who was threatening miscarriage of a child she'd never mentioned to us! I didn't even know what to pray.

But I had already prayed for reconciliation.

My hurt and anger were very real and present. I was confused as to what direction to take in this situation. So I simply said, "If they release you in the morning, call, and one of us will pick you up." I left for home.

The next morning the ride home was quiet. Neither of us knew where to begin. Questions floated in the air, but I couldn't grasp the right one to ask. Silence. An uneasy truce. As we approached her home, I said, "We'll have Giraurd home by 5:00 P.M." She said, "Thanks."

I wrestled with my feelings. I talked with Chuck. I continued to pray. And Saturday night I met with a group of clergy sisters. "What does the word 'forgiveness' mean? How do you act when you forgive?" I wish I had time and space to detail our extended conversation. But what stuck in my spirit was the reality that if I really wanted to forgive my daughter, I would have to let go of my dreams for her life and fully accept her.

How do you give up even your unrealistic expectations for your child's life? How do you withdraw the years of emotional investment? How do you accede to their life choices and love them when you know they are headed for more danger? I really don't have the answers! I just know that involvement in the life of my daughter and grandson meant I had to change. The burden of change was not on her. I had been given this ministry of reconciliation. Now what?

I began to earnestly pray for guidance. I stated to pay particular attention to my feelings and thoughts about Grian. I talked to Chuck, trying to figure out this new process we were moving through. I shared my confusion with trusted friends and with my congregation.

The Wednesday before Christmas, Grian, her boyfriend, and Giraurd stopped by the house. As the baby played in his room, the four of us sat and talked. Questions were asked. Listening was intentional. We asked forgiveness for past hurts. And I stated what was truth for me.

I was honest about my pain. I was open about my wanting to have her and Giraurd in my life. I was also clear that new ground rules had to be laid down. Forgiving doesn't make you a fool! It does make you cautious and tentative, for the pain is real. And you are not ready to bring this potential for additional pain onto the center stage of your life. When forgiveness occurs, a new relationship is established. Trust has to be developed again.

Tough love said that Giraurd couldn't come back into our home without us having legal custody. We would not allow Grian to do further damage to our hearts. I faced the truth. She was not stable. She could yet be involved with drugs. Yet she was an adult. She was his mother.

Letting go of my control was the basic issue for me in our relationship. Giving up my "dream life" for my daughter and facing the truth was not easy. I'm still her mother. And I feel that I know more than she does! Putting limits on my interactions with Giraurd was the most difficult piece of this puzzle. But the road to forgiveness and reconciliation was in sight. It was a very Merry Christmas!

A Quilt for Sistahs

Having been transformed she is surrounded
by a royal clan of queens
a colony of survivors
like a toddler she learns to crawl
then walk as she drops her buckets
of hate/unforgivableness/pain
She drops them down
only to pull up rivers of living water

DEBORAH TINSLEY TAYLOR

PRAYER

Flaming Fire of Love, I give thanks with joy for the miracles you continue to work within this heart of mine. My desire is to take back my yesterdays and to look with great expectation and anticipation to what is ahead for me tomorrow. I praise you for the journey. Never did I think I would say this, for the pain has been so great. Yet I am growing to understand that pain is a purifier of the human spirit. I do not enjoy the pain of yesterday, but your love is helping me to see more than the hurt. I am growing. I am stretching wings. I am seeing hope. I am daring to envision the future.

PSALM 42:1-5

Like the deer that yearns

for running streams,

so my soul is yearning

for you, my God.

My soul is thirsting for God, the living

God.

When can I enter to see the face of God?

My tears have become my food night and

day,

and I hear it said all day long:

"Where is your God?"

I will remember all these things

as I pour out my soul:

how I would lead the joyous procession

into the house of God,

with cries of gladness and thanksgiving,

the multitude wildly happy.

Why are you so sad, my soul?

Why sigh within me?

Hope in God;

for I will yet praise my Savior and my God.

FROM *PSALMS ANEW*

PRINCIPLE

THE OLD, DESTRUCTIVE ANGER WHICH
HELD YOU BACK WILL BE CONVERTED,
TRANSFORMED, AND CHANGED INTO
NEW HEALING ENERGY FOR YOURSELF
AND FOR OTHERS. "THIS IS WHAT THE
SOVEREIGN LORD SAYS, COME FROM
THE FOUR WINDS, O BREATH, AND
BREATHE INTO THESE DRY BONES, THAT
THEY MAY LIVE" (EZEKIEL 37:9).

You are changed! Miracles do happen! The old,
destructive anger is being converted and transformed into a new healing energy for yourself
and others. The elements of wind and thunder
are powers that move you in spite of yourself.
This is the God-force within. "I've found God
inside of me and I love her fiercely," said Celie
in *The Color Purple*. Every social movement in
the world started when people began to focus

their anger-energy into purposeful and helpful
acts for the good of all. It's action time! What
good can your old anger be used for?

CONSIDER

What are the unrealistic expectations you are holding against the person you need to forgive? When you release him or her with your forgiveness, you will be free to change and you allow that person the opportunity to change also!

What is the actual power struggle about between your significant person and yourself?

What are some of the ways you can begin to give up control of, yet still care about, the significant person in your life?

It was not until Mother Rosa Parks got tired and sat down that others stood up and went into action! When you withdraw your "emotional control" over others, what might they begin to do for themselves?

WEEK'S REFLECTIVE REVIEW

What has the Spirit of Life spoken to me this
    week?

This week I have chosen to do at least one thing
    differently. What is the Spirit of Life calling
    me to do?

What has the Spirit of Life taught me this week?

What are my goals for next week's gift of life?

What has the Spirit of Life inspired me to try?

What accomplishments do I celebrate this week?

Many instances and people have been blessings to
    my life this week. What am I especially grate-
    ful for?

CLOSING PRAYER

"Breathe on me, Breath of God, fill me with life anew, that I may love what thou dost love and do what thou wouldst do. Breathe on me, Breath of God, until my heart is pure, until with thee I will one will, to do and to endure."

EDWIN HATCH, 1878

6

GATHERING MY HEALING STONES

I want to take my medicine bag,
those healing stones
that helped me survive your cruelty.

VALERIE J. BRIDGEMAN DAVIS

I have received a command to bless;
God has blessed and I cannot change it.

NUMBERS 23:20

PRINCIPLE

YOU HAVE THE POWER TO BLESS YOUR-
SELF AND OTHERS!

"What do you mean you're letting him come
back home? Are you a fool?" He had hurt her

tremendously. He had played her like a fiddle.
All of us, her friends, knew the many tears she
had shed as he "did his thing" and humiliated
her around the city. I had breathed a sigh of
relief when he had left on a trip "home" and
just didn't come back. She was better off alone!
Who needed constant and unending misery?

The marriage had never been a good one.
She was in too much of a hurry in the first
place. She was middle-aged, the mother of adult
children, well established in the city, and a
respected leader in her church. She was politi-
cally active, financially sound, and socially con-
nected. He didn't bring any of this to the table.
He was simply a younger man. Not a good-
looking, well built, and economically sound
man at that! But he had a line going, she fell for
it, and they got married.

She was into church and all of the educational ministries. He was into running the

streets, playing the horses, and chasing women. She was into the missionary work of the church, doing for others and helping where she could. He was into doing in others and taking from whomever was available. And Sistergirl tried to make it work. She put on a "happy face." She held her peace. She tried not to see. But her heart clearly told her reality.

The pains in her heart became severe. The palpitations were erratic. The fatigue was over-whelming. The doctors put her on medical leave. Her social and church life were curtailed. Her new activities became centered around doctors, heart specialists, and the drugstore.

The more ill she became, the more of a fool he acted. The more she needed his companion-ship and support, the more he stayed away from home. The winds and thunder of her life seemed to be moving against her with raging force. And now her health was betraying her.

She couldn't talk to her blood sister, who simply wanted to hire someone to kill him! She didn't want to share her pain with her aging mother. Since I was both a pastor in town and her sister-friend, we talked and we cried together. I knew the story of her distressing past relationships with other men. I knew the history of her father, who was in her life too little and did not make her feel special, unique, and loved. Disappointments, failures, and setbacks were familiar to her. She had accepted them as a way of life. Yet she held on to her faith. She felt that she had a purpose and a higher destiny in life. She felt that God was calling her to a new level of living.

I listened to her story. This is the real reason we have friends. They listen to us as we unfurl the mysteries of our lives. Friends don't judge, don't condemn, and don't criticize. They stand with you and they ask hard questions.

"Help me to understand. Why you are accepting this abuse?" A hard question. For surely I could not comprehend any woman allowing any man to literally "break her heart!" Others had stayed in Heartbreak Hotel, but she didn't have to go there. And I couldn't see her making a permanent home there.

We talked. We prayed. We wrestled with how Scripture applied to her immediate situation. She began to look at him as a "soul" in need of salvation. But I believe this was her way of saving her sanity. For when you surrender unrealistic expectations and begin to see the truth, you can make decisions based on facts, not fantasy. I saw him as a man who needed a swift kick in the butt. My motto was "kick him out!" Her motto was, "You can never do a kindness too soon. For you never know when it will be too late." A light bulb came on for me! Could this be redemptive, life-producing suffering that God was taking her through? Were there life lessons that she, I, and her women associates were to learn as we journeyed with her down this long and winding road? Could there really be some purpose in this relationship different from what we humans could perceive? I discovered that she was in touch with a higher Consciousness. Discernment was at work within her. God's plan for her was being worked out in this situation which I could not understand. She was not just another woman determined to "stand by her man." She was a woman who was determined to remain in the perfect will of God. It's mighty good to know when God is giving guidance and direction to you.

What my sister-friend was teaching me was extreme kindness in the face of suffering. She decided to operate on a higher plane. She was able to exhibit a heart of compassion. She was the Christ-figure in the life of this needy soul. She supplied loving care to one who was undeserving! She began to internalize and live out of the scripture "Love your enemy. Do good to those who despitefully use you!" Holding on to unforgivableness was not her answer. "Tit for tat" was not a game she was going to play. She decided to stand in the midst of seeming death and ask the same old biblical question, "God, can these bones live?" The answer the prophet gave was, "Lord, only you know!"

"He's still my husband!" The man had gotten intensely ill while away. The doctors had given him six months to live. And he had called my friend, wanting and needing to return. She let him! I couldn't believe it, didn't want to hear it, and had little comprehension of or tolerance for her reasoning. I tried to talk her out of it. I got angry with her. And I went past the pastor-friend relationship and got directly into her business. "Girl, if he's going to die, let him die with his mama!"

Well he came back to live in her home again. He seemed so repentant. He acted so nice. He talked like he had some sense. But realize that he was ill, and in her own medical condition, she reached out to take care of him.

Have you ever heard the story of the individual walking down an icy way who hears a viper asking for help? The person spies a half-frozen viper while walking over to see what's going on. The viper asks to be put in a pocket for warmth. The human looks at the viper in disbelief! "Why would I put you in my pocket? You're a dangerous snake." The snake replies, "But I would never hurt anyone who helps me." You already know the rest of the story. After the snake is put in the pocket and begins to warm and thaw, the individual feels that deadly bite. "Why?" "Because it's my nature," replies the snake.

Boyfriend did not die in six months nor in the next year. The same old story began to be replayed. Women, whispering on the phone, mystery charges appearing on credit card bills, even the suspicion of a child! And my sister kept caring and kept her promise to let him stay. Every time he acted a fool, showed out, and hurt her, she gave his "account" over into the hands of God. She believed that "vengeance belonged to the Lord" and not to her. She felt that this was a mission assignment and she was not going to get an "incomplete."

When his health took a severe decline, she was right there. She diligently followed his care plan and spent long hours sitting at the hospital. When released, the old, repentant spirit returned and he wanted to "do something with his life." He began to attend church with her.

He gave his life to Christ and announced a call to ministry. He decided to open his own business, and guess who was there every day? He even bought a new house and put both of their names on it. She was feeling less stress. I was feeling more suspicious!

As he gained strength, those old habits returned! Trips up and down the road started again. Hidden charge account slips were discovered again. New bills for women's jewelry and clothing turned up again. She was finally fed up and began to look for an apartment. But she heard the voice of God in prayer saying, "Hold steady."

The women's support group was there for her. She remained an active participant in the life of the church and community. Early morning walks helped clear her head. The ability to cry and to vent were assets. Teaching Sunday school and preparing sermons made her dig

into the Scriptures and the Living Word spoke
to her. She began to travel with her sister and to
visit her children in different cities. These
became her "healing stones." These activities
helped her to maintain her sanity. The ability to
share her life with other women allowed both
her and them to see the spiritual growth which
this time of great testing was bringing to her
life. She was not simply wasting her life, but living fully, sharing herself and her resources. She
was available to minister to him, but she had
withdrawn her emotional energy from him. No
longer did she expect or anticipate that he
would change or become what she needed. In
these ways she could cope and remain loving in
her ministry to him as they continued to live
and run the business together.

Two months after hearing God say, "Hold
steady," he returned from a road trip to buy
supplies, sat on a corner of the couch, and died.

She was free. She had completed her mission to him. She had a clear conscience. She had been blessed by God and had truly been a blessing to him. She had survived all of his cruelty by living out the many lessons of faith she had gathered along life's way. She didn't do what I or her sister would have done. She held steady and followed the course outlined for her journey by the Divine. In so doing she modeled how to take back yesterday in order to move into a better tomorrow.

A Note

Many things I could not say
This has not been a place of rest
But I continue each day.
I fill my days with many things,
including times to offer praise.
Nothing has really gotten any better,
but then that's not entirely true.

I keep washing my hair, do my nails,
smile at old folks and kiss babies.
I will get through!

LETTER FROM
DEBBIE TINSLEY TAYLOR

PRAYER

I know that at times I will be troubled,
I know that at times I will be belabored,
I know that at times I will be disquieted,
but I believe that I will not be overcome. Amen.

JULIAN OF NORWICH,
ENGLAND, 1342–1419

To "know" God is to have an intimate relationship. It is to be open to being with, receiving
from, sharing with, and giving in return to the
generous God who loves you. What is it that
you "know" about your journey with God to
take back your yesterday?

PSALM 91:8–15

Behold, look with your own eyes

and see the punishment of the wicked—

because you have God for your refuge.

You have made the Most High your

stronghold.

No harm shall befall you,

nor shall any affliction come near your tent;

God has commanded angels

to guard you in all your ways.

In their hands they shall raise you up

so that you will not hurt your foot against a

stone.

You shall tread upon the lion and the viper;

you shall trample the lion and the dragon.

"Because you cling to me, I will deliver you;

I will protect you because you acknowledge

my name.

You shall call upon me and I will answer

you.

I will be with you in times of trouble;
I will deliver you and glorify you
and will show you my salvation."

FROM *PSALMS ANEW*

How have you been able to recognize God in
the pain of your yesterday?

PRINCIPLE

> YOU HAVE THE POWER TO BLESS YOURSELF
> AND OTHERS! "I HAVE RECEIVED A COM-
> MAND TO BLESS; GOD HAS BLESSED AND I
> CANNOT CHANGE IT" (NUMBERS 23:20).

Go ahead, say it! "I am a blessing! I have to bless others! I don't have a choice! God made me a blessing!" Isn't it awesome! Doesn't it feel good way down on the inside? Regardless of what you have felt about yourself in the midst of your unforgivableness, God says you are a blessing! You are not bad, horrible, worthless, or unsaved! You are a gift, a favored child, and approved of by God. Is this affirmation or what? This is the time you can receive validation from others. Share the story of your healing journey. Be a witness over a cup of tea, flavored coffee, or mineral water. Bless someone else with the present of yourself. Who will be first?

CONSIDER

Touch your forehead and bless yourself. Touch
your eyes and bless yourself. Touch your mouth
and bless yourself. Touch your feet and bless
yourself. Do it on a daily basis. It's time to learn
how to lay healing hands on yourself and on
others. You are a blessing to yourself! Beauti-
cians and nail technicians touch us and we feel
special. It's a soothing touch that they give, and
we need to attend to ourselves with the same
tenderness. Go ahead, hug yourself. What do
you experience as you "lay hands" on yourself?

A brand new attitude means it's make-over
time! New makeup, new outfit, new shoes, new
hose color, and new underclothes. Yes, new
nightclothes. So what if you sleep alone. You are
still a queen! Look the part from top to bottom.
Perfumes, aromatherapy, bath oils and beads are

methods of self-healing. The items don't have to be super-expensive. Just a little somethin' somethin', even from the Goodwill Boutique, will establish a new healing moment in time for you!

I wear purple silk underwear! I shop for them relentlessly. (They're hard to find.) Purple is the color of African royalty. Purple is the color Lydia sold in Scripture. Purple is a regal color symbolizing my being a daughter of the Most High God. I wear silk undies to have something soft and sensuous next to my body. Regardless of what happens during the day, no matter what mess I make or encounter, despite what some knucklehead says to the contrary, I feel royal and regal! Purple underwear has become a healing balm for me. What can you use to "wrap yourself in healing" all day long?

What "healing stones" have you learned
from your past which will help you to get
through any situation? Can you name the
growth in your medicine bag that has been a
direct result of your painful yesterday? (This is
the purpose of redemptive or "growing" pain!)

WEEK'S REFLECTIVE REVIEW

What has the Spirit of Life spoken to me this
week?

This week I have chosen to do at least one thing
differently. What is the Spirit of Life calling
me to do?

What has the Spirit of Life taught me this week?

What are my goals for next week's gift of life?

What has the Spirit of Life inspired me to try?

What accomplishments do I celebrate this week?

Many instances and people have been blessings to
my life this week. What am I especially grateful for?

CLOSING PRAYER

Wellspring of Joy, new life bubbles within me. You have allowed me to glimpse hints of your purpose in all of my painful yesterdays. I continue to have questions about why. I continue to wish it had never happened to me. And yet some of the nonsense is beginning to make more sense to me. Many pieces of the puzzle of my life are starting to fall into place. Thank you for healing stones which will help me in my tomorrow. May it be so now and always.

7
TAKING BACK MY YESTERDAYS

All you stole, I now reclaim with force.
VALERIE J. BRIDGEMAN DAVIS

*So if you think you are standing
firm, be careful that you don't fall.*
1 CORINTHIANS 10:12

PRINCIPLE

FORGIVENESS MEANS THAT I REALIZE
MY OWN HUMANNESS AS WELL AS THAT
OF THE ONE WHO HAS VICTIMIZED ME.

Helena never thought she would be in this
place. She was bereft. She felt despondent. She
felt like she was dying. She wanted to die. She

123

was black. She was a single mom. She was
unemployed. And now she was homeless!
Helena never thought this could happen to
her. She had done the "right" things. She was
a decent woman. She was a hard worker. She
had proven skills. She had tried so hard. Yet she
was in this wilderness place, a shelter for the
homeless.

This was supposed to have been her time.
She was an orphan who had gone on to further
her education so that she could take care of
herself. The position which paid her salary and
provided a nicely furnished apartment was not
very challenging, but she had a decent roof over
her head. Then she had answered that stupid
advertisement. A couple had needed a surrogate
mother and was willing to pay an unbelievable
price. She had been selected from among the
applicants. She felt blessed to have this opportunity to move into a better neighborhood, to

leave the boring job, and to wait as life formed within her womb.

She had spent the months reading, visiting art galleries and museums, listening to chamber music, trying to ensure that the baby had the very best environment to develop. Those had been good days.

The couple had been supportive. They seemed excited. The monthly stipend was always on time and every need she had was met. They had not been haughty and overbearing, but treated her like family. She had spent time with them, answering their many questions about her and her background. Finally the time had come and the birth had not been difficult at all. The hospital notified the couple, but neither one of them showed up. She had undergone the labor alone. She had delivered with ease and told the staff she did not want to see the child. They had put her in a private room and she had awaited the couple's arrival. They had never come. The man showed up the next morning alone.

"My wife has left me! She wants no part of this child and feels that I pressured her into this arrangement. I'm sorry, but I can't take the child. You will have to figure out a way yourself. My marriage is at stake. I hope you understand."

There was nothing to do except collect her child and return to the apartment which was too small for company. She had nothing for the child. This was to have been their role. Now she had no job, no income, and a baby that she didn't know what to do with. When the month was up, she and the baby were put out of the building. The social service worker had referred them to the shelter.

Helena never thought she would be in this place. She was bereft. She was despondent. She felt like she was dying. She wanted to die. She was black. She was a single mom. She was unemployed. Now she was homeless! Helena never thought this could happen to her. Yet she was in a wilderness place.

The wilderness is a place that each one of us will travel. The wilderness is known to everyone. For the wilderness is a call to new decisions, different choices and different directions. The wilderness is simply a metaphor for indecision, lack of direction, unclear focus, and generally being lost.

The question is not, "Have you ever been lost in the wilderness?" The question is, "How did you survive while you were in the wilderness?" For wilderness times and wilderness experiences will sap your energy, steal your joy, and leave you, like Helena, bereft, despondent, and depressed.

Helena is a fictional character who helps us to see just how unfair life can treat us in these times in which we live. And she has a biblical counterpart who helps us to understand how to deal with our wilderness experiences of pain, abandonment, and anxiety. Her name is Hagar, an Egyptian woman of color who was a slave to Mr. Abraham and Mrs. Sarah.

Hagar did what she was told. She went where she was told. Her field of choices was very narrow. So when Sarah decided that Hagar would have sex with Abraham, conceive by Abraham, and bear a child for her and Abraham, Sistergirl did as she was told.

One day, while Hagar was playing with her own infant, who technically belonged to her owners, Sarah got an attitude with Hagar. Hagar had done her job. She did just what she was told. She had fulfilled her assignment and now she was being a good mother. This says that being found in the wilderness is not always your fault. Being lost, wandering in a dry place, is not always a direct correlation to your wrongdoing or stupidity. You can do the right thing, follow orders to the letter, obey directions perfectly, and still find yourself in the middle of the wilderness.

Sarah told Abraham that she wanted nothing to do with this woman and her baby. Hagar was put out, kicked to the curb, dissed with her child! Black, slave, homeless, unemployed, and a single mom, Hagar found herself in a difficult space. "So Abraham rose early in the morning, and took bread and a skin of water, and gave it to Hagar, putting it on her shoulder, along with the child, and sent her away. And she departed, and wandered about in the wilderness of Beersheba" (Genesis 21:14).

Have you ever found yourself in a predicament and wondered why it happened? Ever find yourself overwhelmed by an unexpected situation and wondered what you did to deserve it? Ever find yourself in a place where there were few friendly faces and nobody even cared to know your name? And you wonder how you ended up in the middle of the mess? Then you know what it feels like for Ms. Hagar to wander lost in Beer-sheba.

Beer-sheba can be in your house. Beer-sheba can be on your job. Beer-sheba can be your dysfunctional past. Beer-sheba can be your crazy kids. Beer-sheba can be that messed-up relationship. Beer-sheba can be the betrayal of a loved one. For Beer-sheba is just another name for the time of crisis.

Beer-sheba can happen to you so fast that it will make your head swim. There is pain in the wilderness. There is grief in the wilderness. There is loneliness in the wilderness. There is the temptation to hate and never forgive in the wilderness. There is a human bent toward planning for revenge in the wilderness. There is the strong urge to find the easiest way out of the wilderness by blaming others, feeling sorry for yourself, and looking down in contempt upon the one who hurt you. But Hagar teaches us that the wilderness is the place where God will encounter us. The wilderness is the place where God will hear the faintest cry. The wilderness is the place where we can clearly discern the voice of God. And the wilderness is the place where new direction for life will be given.

Hagar threw her son under a tree and went a distance away and sat down and began to weep and wail. We need to separate ourselves from those people who have hurt us. We need to learn how to cultivate quiet, restful times and spaces in our lives. For Hagar teaches us that we can get our hands off the situation. Leave it alone. "Let go and let God," we're told. And if you want to take back your yesterdays, you will learn how to run away, reflect quietly, and search your soul for wholeness.

Then our sister took the time to have a real good cry. Tears relieve stress. Tears uncap bottled frustration. Tears wash away anger and bitterness from our souls. Tears clear our vision and allow us to see life better. Tears are precious unto our God. So go ahead and cry!

What is essential for taking back a yesterday is understanding that you are not alone, even in the wilderness. Your sitting, your intentional silence, and your loud crying are each forms of sincere prayer. And our God hears and answers prayers. God heard the cries of Hagar's little boy and directed an angel to give her instructions for survival in the wilderness.

"Do not be afraid. Lift up the boy, hold him securely. For I will make a great nation out of him" (Genesis 21:18–19). The same promise that Abraham had received, so Hagar received for her son. This slave woman, cast out and thrown away, sent off into the wilderness to die, had received a promise of new and abundant life. The Bible goes on to say that when the promise came, "God opened her eyes and she saw a well of water" (v. 19).

When Hagar heard from God in the wilderness, her spiritual eyes opened. When she heard from God she was able to see the plan God had for her life. When she heard from God, the bigger picture came into view. Her past began to make sense. The answers to all her questions about the hurt, grief, and pain fell into place like pieces of a puzzle. "Oh, I had to come this way that I might hear from God!"

This was not about Abraham and Sarah being no good, unsaved, or evil. This was not even about Hagar being enslaved, mistreated, and hurt. This lesson came that Hagar might realize that she and they were part of God's plan for the world. They were all cut from the same human cloth, with fragilities, liabilities, and a tendency toward doing wrong. In a patriarchal system both Hagar and Sarah were victims. Both were sisters in a system that viewed them as chattel. They were related by gender and by societal expectations. Sarah's actions, although wrong and evil, are consistent with victim behaviors. She identified with the strong, ruling power figure, Abraham, and despised the woman who was more at risk than she. Internally she knew that "there but for the grace of God, go I!"

What Abraham, Sarah, and Hagar did was to be taken care of by God. The wrongs that Abraham and Sarah had committed were on God's record. The pain they had caused Hagar had been noted and duly recorded. But ultimately her life, the life of her son, and their lives were in the capable hands of God. And Hagar had to undergo the pain in order to reap the glory. "Oh, I had to come this way that I might hear from God!" Hagar learned some valuable lessons in her wilderness experience.

The jury is yet out on Helena and you. Hagar took back her yesterday by claiming the power and the promises that God had given unto her and her son. The story concludes with her going on about her business, taking care of her child, and leaving the revenge on Abraham and Sarah up to God! Yes, she felt the pain of rejection, abandonment, and enslavement. Yes, she was left alone with a child to raise. Yes, life was difficult and it was not fair. Yes, she spent time crying, weeping, and wailing. And yes, she heard the voice of God saying to her, "Don't be afraid!"

Sisters, don't be afraid to risk letting go of your pain. Don't be afraid to take the necessary steps to hear God speaking to you in the quiet of your wilderness space. Don't be afraid to let the tears flow and to lift up your voice in lamentation. And don't be afraid to stop crying, get up, and move ahead with your life. For when you decide to do like Hagar and take your hands off of the situation, God can fix it for you.

Hagar becomes the paradigm for taking back our yesterdays when we revisit her story and look at the theological implications of what she took with her as she journeyed into the wilderness. Abraham gave Hagar a loaf of bread and a skin of water to take with her. Jesus claims, "I am the Bread of Life" and "I am the Living Water." In his dying and rising he promised to never leave or forsake us. He went on to promise to send back the Holy Spirit to live in us, to feed us in solitary places, and to spring up inside of us when our well is dry.

You can't take back your yesterdays with human effort alone. But the Bread of Life and the Well of Eternal Waters is available right now. Eat and drink. Yesterday is yours for the taking.

All you stole, I now reclaim with force.
The violence you used against me—
that whirlwind that wrecked my life—
well, I have learned to harness winds and
     thunder.
The violence, I have turned to my own
     power.
And yes, I am here to take everything you
     kept:
pieces of my soul,
parts of my heart.
And my destiny.
The future is ahead, and I need them.
I am taking back my yesterdays.

VALERIE J. BRIDGEMAN DAVIS

PRAYER

Holy Wholeness, the journey has been so long from yesterday to now. It has not been easy to relive the haunting days gone by. Yet your love has sustained me and your Holy Spirit has held me fast. Many times I have felt lost along the paths as they have curved, twisted, and turned in directions I did not want to go. Thank you for bringing me safely and sanely this far. Thank you for helping me to see the benefit of surrender to a better plan than holding on to rage and anger in my heart. I don't know what tomorrow will bring, but I give thanks for what I have reclaimed from yesterday.

PSALM 40:1–3

I waited and waited for you, Yahweh!

Now at last you have turned to me

and heard my cry for help.

You have lifted me out of the horrible

      pit . . .

set my feet on a rock

and steadied my steps.

Yahweh, you have put a new song in my

      mouth—

a song of praise.

Many will look on in awe

and will put their trust in you.

FROM *PSALMS ANEW*

PRINCIPLE

> FORGIVENESS MEANS THAT I REALIZE
> MY OWN HUMANNESS AS WELL AS THAT
> OF THE ONE WHO VICTIMIZED ME. "SO,
> IF YOU THINK YOU ARE STANDING FIRM,
> BE CAREFUL THAT YOU DON'T FALL"
> (1 CORINTHIANS 10:12).

"This is the day of new beginnings!" Today we can acknowledge that we and the victimizer are alike. Of course this is hard to say. Yet both of us are human beings subject to sin. Both of us have human frailties. Both of us hurt and have hurt others. And the capacity for evil is in everyone of us. Can you honestly understand how you are related to the one who hurt you?

CONSIDER

Because you have acquired a new level of sensitivity on this journey, you can realize the many ways you have hurt others in the same way you have been hurt. My father raped me physically. Because we have a human need to identify with "strong, powerful" people and hate weak victims, it is not surprising that I also raped people. The instrument I used was my sharp tongue. In what ways have you done the very thing you hate to others?

You have a full twelve hours to do as you please! Pretend you are going to work. Dress and fix a lunch or buy one on your way. Go to that hotel you have always wanted to spend some time in, check in, and chill till it's time to return home at the end of your "work" day. What will you do with your free day? What do you need to take in your "work" bag? (Don't forget the bath beads!)

Hagar was told, "Do not be afraid." Define your fears. Name what you could do if they were not part of your life. Listen for the inner voice to speak and give directions as to how they can be released.

When Hagar "opened her eyes" she was able to see water that had been there all the time! What is it that you have not been "seeing" which will help you take back your yesterdays?

WEEK'S REFLECTIVE REVIEW

What has the Spirit of Life spoken to me this
    week?

This week I have chosen to do at least one thing
    differently. What is the Spirit of Life calling
    me to do?

What has the Spirit of Life taught me this week?

What are my goals for next week's gift of life?

What has the Spirit of Life inspired me to try?

What accomplishments do I celebrate this week?

Many instances and people have been blessings to
    my life this week. What am I especially grate-
    ful for?

CLOSING PRAYER

Listening Lover, you have entered into my pain and blessed me abundantly. In your gentle presence I have been given hope again in tomorrow. Thank you for being such a present help, making the journey with me into yesterday and bringing me comfort and growth. We go now to continue the process of taking back my yesterdays! May it be so, now and always!

AN AFTERWORD ON FORGIVENESS

My prayer is that some word, some individual, some principle, prayer, psalm, or poem has touched your heart and allowed the thought of forgiveness to form in your mind. If you think about forgiveness, the power of the Holy Spirit has penetrated the hard core formed around your wounded heart. The journey is well under way. Forgiveness is a process and has many different and diverse forms and patterns. Each of the people identified in this book began at various points and moved back and forth as well as around in circles as they moved toward forgiving.

Lewis Smedes's book *The Art of Forgiving* says, "Forgiving happens inside the person who does it . . . as we discover the frail, failed, and bruised humanity of the person we forgive . . .

and welcome them back into the circle of people we care about." Forgiving is about our heart growing tender, being healed and made more loving toward the one we had "killed off," dissed, and banished from our care. Forgiving is finally taking them off of our personal "hit list." However, Smedes hurries on to say, "Forgiving is not about reunion and forgiving does not obligate us to go back!"

Too many times before we have thought about forgiving. And then we denied that thought as we realized that we were not ready for reunion, homecoming, and "happy days." Reunion is another process and another book. In order to restore a relationship, there must also be repentance and amends made on the part of the individual who has done you wrong. Forgiving is what can happen to you as you allow the Holy Spirit to work the miracle of releasing your need for revenge. Keep focused on the goal of forgiving and do not link forgiving with return to the former relationship.

Once again Smedes supplies some necessary clarification: "It takes one person to forgive. It takes two to be reunited. Forgiving happens inside the wounded person. Reunion happens in a relationship between people. . . . We can forgive even if we do not trust the person not to wrong us again. Reunion can happen only if we trust this individual not to wrong us again. Forgiving has no strings attached. Reunion has several strings attached. . . . A person can truly forgive and refuse to be reunited."

The principles of forgiveness work for everybody. It makes no difference what your religious preference or tradition. Forgiveness is that universal principle which draws the best into our world. Forgiveness is the principle of the universe which attracts love, light, and liberty to us. Forgiveness is the principle which uplifts, inspires, motivates, and transforms our lives. These principles are simply stated and yet difficult to put into operation. They require work on our part. They demand practice, practice, and practice. They compel us to listen to the still, small voice within. And they require that most times we act and behave the opposite of what we have "always" done.

Yet we know that unforgiveness keeps us locked in yesterday. Unforgiveness continues to hold us in stagnant, life-defying places. Unforgiveness pulls us down into horrible pits where the muck and the mire almost sucks the life right out of us. It is essential that we begin the healing work of forgiveness. For taking back our yesterdays propels us into better tomorrows with more healthy relationships, less stress, and wholeness for our physical selves. So come on, let's get busy!

BENEDICTION

May the God of the Ancestor's bless you.

May the Ancient of Days enfold you.

May the Light of Glory shine upon you.

May the Darkness of Growth give you rest.

May the Help of the Ages go with you.

May the Hope of Tomorrow help you always

take back your yesterdays!

RESOURCES

Ahlers, Julia, Rosemary Broughton, and Carl
    Koch. *Woman Psalms.* Winona, Minn.:
    Saint Mary's Press, 1992.

Jampolsky, Gerald G., with Patricia Hopkins
    and William Thetford. *Good-Bye to
    Guilt.* New York: Bantam Books, 1985.

Klug, Lyn. *Soul Weavings.* Minneapolis:
    Augsburg Fortress, 1996.

Miller, D. Patrick. *A Little Book of Forgiveness.*
    New York: Viking Press, 1994.

Schreck, Nancy, and Maureen Leach. *Psalms
    Anew.* Winona, Minn.: Saint Mary's
    Press, 1986.

Simon, Sidney B., and Suzanne Simon.
    Forgiveness. New York: Warner Books,
    1990.
Smedes, Lewis B. *The Art of Forgiving.*
    Nashville: Moorings Press, 1996.